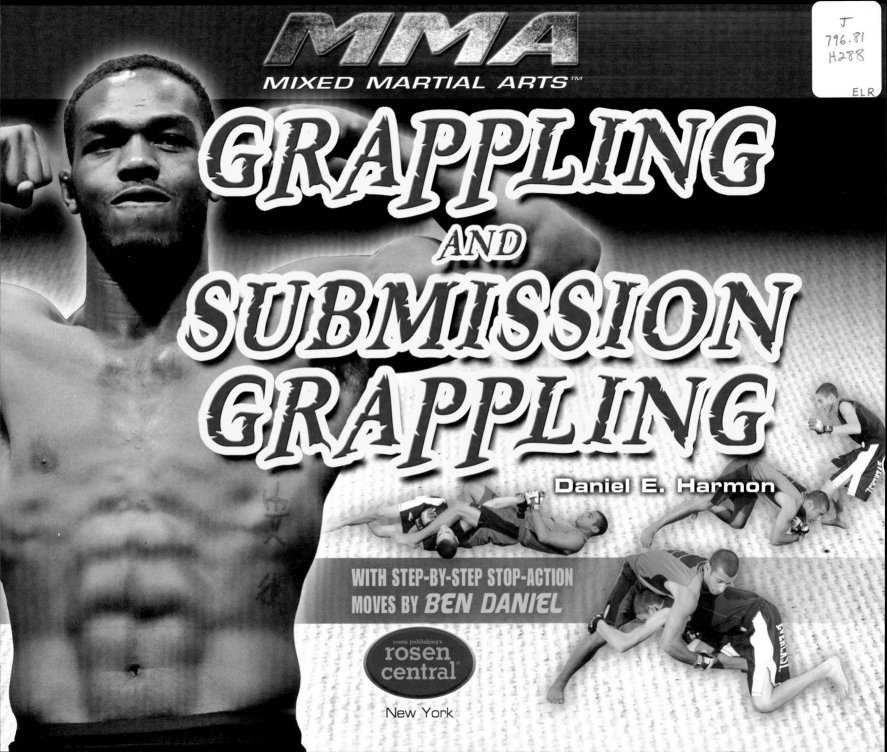

MMA
MIXED MARTIAL ARTS™

GRAPPLING
AND
SUBMISSION GRAPPLING

Daniel E. Harmon

WITH STEP-BY-STEP STOP-ACTION
MOVES BY *BEN DANIEL*

rosen publishing's
rosen central®

New York

Dedicated to my loving Sensei, Master Mal Perkins, 6th dan. This wouldn't have come to fruition without the love and training you have given me over the years. Hail, Master Mal! —Ben Daniel

Published in 2013 by The Rosen Publishing Group, Inc.
29 East 21st Street, New York, NY 10010

Copyright © 2013 by The Rosen Publishing Group, Inc.

First Edition

Description of moves by Sensei Ben Daniel.

This book is published only as a means of providing information on unique aspects of the history and current practice of martial arts. Neither Rosen Publishing nor the author makes any representation, warranty, or guarantee that the techniques described or photographs included in this book will be safe or effective in any self-defense situation or otherwise. You may be injured if you apply or train in the techniques of self-defense presented in this book, and neither Rosen Publishing nor the author is responsible for any such injury that may result. It is essential that you consult a parent or guardian regarding whether or not to attempt any technique described in this book. Specific self-defense techniques shown in this book may not be called for in a specific set of circumstances or under applicable federal, state, or local law. Neither Rosen Publishing nor the author makes any representation or warranty regarding the legality or appropriateness of any technique mentioned in this book.

Library of Congress Cataloging-in-Publication Data

Harmon, Daniel E.
Grappling and submission grappling/Daniel E. Harmon.
    p. cm.—(MMA: Mixed martial arts)
Includes bibliographical references and index.
ISBN 978-1-4488-6964-0 (library binding)
1. Hand-to-hand fighting. 2. Mixed martial arts. I. Title.
GV1111.H283 2012
796.81—dc23

2011051025

Manufactured in the United States of America

CPSIA Compliance Information: Batch #S12YA: For further information, contact Rosen Publishing, New York, New York, at 1-800-237-9932.

 CONTENTS

At least a hundred million people around the world engage in different forms of martial arts. Not all of them enjoy fighting. The term "martial" suggests combat. But at their historical roots, most martial art systems have peaceful purposes. They were developed for physical fitness, self-discipline, and relaxing the mind and body.

Some martial art forms are not as well known in the United States as in other countries. Millions of Chinese, for example, practice t'ai chi, a form of kung fu, for exercise, relaxation, and meditation. It includes slow, graceful, dance-like movements performed in unbroken sequence.

Fighters touch gloves at the beginning of a round in a mixed martial arts bout. After the courteous formality, almost anything goes in an MMA contest.

The main forms of modern martial arts are kung fu, karate, and tae kwon do. Other systems are based on them. Among the special forms are jiu-jitsu, aikido, and judo. For thousands of years, different cultures have practiced systems of concentrated movement and bodily combat techniques. These skills, while intended first for exercise and meditation, have been useful in warfare and self-defense, too.

Observers interested in martial arts for combat purposes long have wondered: Which fighting system is superior? Can a wrestler withstand the blows of a boxer long enough to move in for a chokehold? Can a karate expert subdue a jiu-jitsu master with kicks and chops before being gripped and thrown to the mat?

By the late 1900s, commercial fight promoters believed money could be made finding out the answers. They began presenting experts of different fighting systems in mixed-arts contests.

The first mixed-form bouts pitted one specialist against another—a sumo wrestler against a kickboxer, for instance. For a brief time, that excited audiences who wanted to know if one was the "ultimate" fighting system. Soon, spectators became interested not so much in systems as in individual fighters. Many fighters were studying and learning to combine techniques from multiple fighting forms.

A new sport, mixed martial arts (MMA), was born. In MMA, a fighter can try most anything against an opponent. The contestant can punch like a boxer or kick and chop like a karate expert. The fighter can use grabbing, grappling, throwing, choking, and other moves common in wrestling.

Twenty-first-century mixed martial artists blend all of the fighting techniques. Unless they can subdue an opponent with fist and elbow blows and kicks, fighters have to win in close quarters, usually on the mat. They must be first-rate grapplers. Superiority in submission grappling techniques greatly improves their likelihood of winning an MMA fight.

Female as well as male grapplers test their physical and mental abilities at the Pan American Games and other competitions.

From the early years of MMA, critics have voiced shock at the exceptional violence. Fighters get hurt. Some fights are very bloody. The same is true in boxing and other long-accepted contact sports, but MMA has come under particular scrutiny by lawmakers. Three states ban public MMA events.

Mixed martial arts got its negative reputation during the early 1990s. It was advertised as a "blood sport." Many spectators who paid to see fights via pay-per-view TV were literally bloodthirsty.

This brand of raw appeal is nothing new. For centuries, people betted on bare-knuckle boxing matches that sometimes resulted in permanent injury and death. Professional wrestling has entertained audiences since the 1930s and is a big-money entertainment medium today. The bloodier the better, in the minds of some fans.

Many of the punches, kicks, holds, and locks seen in professional wrestling resemble techniques used in MMA. But there is a basic difference. Professional wrestling is a scripted show. Promoters and writers decide beforehand how long a match will last, who will win, and what the winning move will be. The outrageous antics of popular wrestlers are exercises in acting. Pro wrestling requires physical excellence and skill and can be dangerous, but most injuries are faked.

Not so in mixed martial arts. Fighters' intensity is genuine. Kicks and punches really hurt. Blood streaming from faces is real.

Spokesmen for the Ultimate Fighting Championship (UFC), the leading MMA organizer, allow that some spectators want to see violence. But they argue that mixed martial arts has matured. Discipline, hard work, and safety are central to the sport. So is mutual respect among fighters.

Mixed martial arts has become extremely popular and is finding new broadcast platforms. Eric Shanks, president of Fox Sports, has called it "the fastest-growing sport in the world."

Significantly, the sport especially attracts male fans ages eighteen to thirty-four. But the number of younger enthusiasts is multiplying. Advocates argue that mixed martial arts—carefully supervised—is safer for children than football, gymnastics, and certain other sports.

In general, "grappling" is the same as "wrestling." Grappling techniques are rooted in the most ancient forms of wrestling. They have become more sophisticated through the centuries. Sophisticated grappling moves have been incorporated into the wrestling systems of different cultures.

The International Federation of Associated Wrestling Styles (FILA) regulates international grappling competition. By FILA's definition, modern-day submission grappling, or "submission wrestling," entails forcing an opponent into submission (surrendering) without striking.

For young athletes excited by the MMA phenomenon, grappling is just one part of what they must master. Most aspiring fighters do not learn grappling techniques because they want to become grappling champions. Rather, they want to become mixed martial arts champions. Top grapplers are known primarily for their success in Brazilian jiu-jitsu, judo, Greco-Roman wrestling, or another fighting form. Regardless, any MMA fighter who wants to succeed must develop excellent grappling skills.

CHAPTER 1

UNDERSTANDING GRAPPLING AND SUBMISSION GRAPPLING

Mixed martial arts encompass thousands of carefully practiced moves. Hundreds of these moves are grappling techniques.

To an unknowing viewer watching a match, what appears to be a single action may be a combination of moves. They all are carried out in a split second.

BASIC GRAPPLING TECHNIQUES

Clinching is a mutual tie-up where two standing fighters join at close quarters. They lock arms in different ways, contorting their bodies and gripping for advantage. From a clinch, a fighter hopes to find a way to take down and overpower the rival with punches or a submission move. Clinching sometimes is a defensive tactic used to buy time against a stronger or more skilled opponent. Training in wrestling and judo develops clinching skills.

In a UFC lightweight title match, a competitor maneuvers a sudden takedown. Fighters hope they will land in an advantageous mount position. A takedown may be the culmination of a carefully planned combination of lightning moves.

In this UFC bout, the contestant on the bottom is pinned—momentarily, at least. Once the fight goes to the mat, it becomes mainly a contest of grappling skills.

A takedown is one of many moves that literally take the fight to the mat from a standing position. In mixed martial arts, fighters who are better at grappling than striking are especially eager to get the fight on the mat. The sooner they do, the sooner they can quell the opponent's barrage of blows and bring their own strengths into play.

Taking the battle to the ground does not assure the outcome. The fighter on the bottom at any given moment can end up on top in the blink of an eye. However, it is to a grappler's advantage to land on top immediately after a takedown. For that reason, clinchers consider carefully which takedown method they will try.

A typical takedown attempt is a leg sweep. In a sudden, powerful side sweep with a foot, a grappler can kick the legs from under the opponent.

Single- and double-leg throws are common takedown techniques. Although the names suggest the moves are similar, they are quite different. In a single-leg throw, the fighter manages to hook (trap) one of the opponent's legs behind the ankle and driving forward, force the opponent backward to the mat. In a double-leg throw, the fighter suddenly goes low, grabs both the opponent's legs, and tackles the opponent to the ground.

In a hip throw, a fighter's legs are planted so that the hips are the center of gravity. The opponent's upper body is thrown across a hip onto the mat.

There are more adventurous takedown techniques such as the fireman's carry. The name comes from the well-known image of a firefighter or battlefield soldier hefting a wounded comrade across the shoulders and carrying the victim to safety. The difference in MMA is that the victim is about to be thrown to the ground.

Fighters attempting a takedown don't rely on just one move. They plan a combination of two, three, and even four throwing moves. If they fail in an initial attack from the right, for example, they are prepared to instantly unleash an attempt from a different direction. This is part of the mental challenge of MMA. Fighters constantly try to surprise their opponents with unexpected combinations.

An ideal result of a takedown is to achieve a mount. A full mount position is straddling the midsection of an opponent who is lying back-down on the mat. In a back mount, the fighter on the bottom is facedown. In a side mount, both fighters are prone, but one has control over the other's upper body.

Although not a position of submission, the mount puts a fighter in control. From a full

Outside of mixed martial arts, grappling competitions are held internationally. The Abu Dhabi Combat Club (ADCC) sponsors the annual Submission Wrestling World Championship. Accomplished professionals in judo, jui-jitsu, wrestling, sambo, and other martial arts compete.

FILA (the International Federation of Associated Wrestling Styles) is an organization that regulates grappling competition. It establishes age and weight divisions and defines rules about dominant positions, illegal holds and moves, and submission terms and signals.

mount, the fighter has great freedom to rain down fist blows, which may result in submission or in the referee stopping the fight. The fighter who gains a full mount may employ other submission tactics.

MMA fighters must know how to take down the opponent with advantage. At the same time, they must know how to defend against a takedown. The most common defense against a double-leg throw, for example, is the sprawl. Basically, sprawling is keeping the legs placed firmly apart.

When fighters fail to avoid a throw, they may be able to roll in such a way that they end up on top. Fighters practice variations of rolls and falls.

They also know how to control a fight even while on their backs. They can do this with what are called guard techniques, using their legs to fend off the opponent.

Sometimes fighters find themselves struggling on their knees. An attacking technique used frequently in this situation is the arm drag. Hooking an arm, a grappler throws the opponent to the mat.

Experienced fighters know how to escape from most problem positions. The basic escape from a full mount, for instance, is simple (at least in theory). The victim hooks a leg over the back of one of the assailant's heels on the floor and rolls in that direction. If it works, the fighter who controlled the mount a moment ago now ends up on the bottom.

SUBMISSION GRAPPLING MOVES

When the fight is taken to the ground, grapplers struggle for a submission hold. Common submission holds include a variety of chokes and limb locks.

Some chokeholds are strangles, cutting off the opponent's air. Others interrupt blood flow. Probably the most famous MMA chokehold is the rear naked choke. A fighter from behind gets an arm around the opponent's neck. The crook of the elbow exerts pressure under the chin while the attacker, with the opposite hand, pushes forward against the back of the victim's head.

Arm bars and arm locks frequently win MMA contests. Some holds exert so much pressure on joints that major injury could result if the victim does not submit. Others simply immobilize the opponent.

Over the years, grapplers have devised many variations of limb locks. In a technique called the Americana, a fighter from a side mount position uses both forearms to trap one of the opponent's wrists. The opponent, back to the mat, is pinned and helpless.

TRAINING

Although fighters are known for their prowess in a particular fighting style, they must train in other styles, too. Meanwhile, they keep their bodies in top condition. They lift weights and put themselves through other strength-training regimens and agility exercises.

A strict diet is fundamental. In his book *Drill to Win*, grappling expert André Galvão commits the entire first month of his year-long training program to learning "the Diet of a Champion."

Professional mixed martial artists are constantly in training. Besides muscle strengthening, they spar with other fighters, perfecting attacks and defenses. Coaches point out their mistakes.

Galvão declares that sticking to a proper diet "is one of the hardest parts of your journey to better jiu-jitsu. You must train your mind to have the willpower to eat what you need for success and to say no to the dessert after dinner!"

CHAPTER 2

STARS OF GRAPPLING AND SUBMISSION GRAPPLING

All competitors in mixed martial arts must devote some of their training time to grappling techniques. The leading grapplers give these tactics special attention, perfecting takedowns, submission holds, and secondary moves. They also become the best escape artists. Career-changing moments for an MMA professional may hinge on the ability to secure a grappling submission—or the inability to avoid one.

Training for submission grapplers is highly intense. Fighters greatly respect top coaches. André Galváo has remarked that while training with Leo Vieira in 2006–2008, "every class was like a seminar to me. . . I felt fortunate to see jiu-jitsu being created right in front of me."

André Galvão is a formidable kicker and striker but is noted especially for his mastery of grappling techniques. He emphasizes the need for dedicated training and diet for success.

ANDRÉ GALVÃO

André Galvão was born in 1982 in São Sebastian, Brazil. He learned judo as a child. Influenced by the interest and training of an older brother, he began to study Brazilian jiu-jitsu and submission wrestling techniques. Today, he is considered one of the best in the world in both categories.

Galvão does not consider himself an exceptionally gifted athlete. He attributes most of his success to hard work.

Galvão received special encouragement from his father. The family was poor. Galvão and his two teenage brothers had to work, sacrificing their training. When Galvão was seventeen, his father agreed to work extra to support their BJJ ambitions—on one condition, "to ensure that we took it seriously." They had to win championships. Galvão was determined to win, and he understood that a ticket to victory could be bought only with hard work.

He won his first tournament as a BJJ white belt with his favorite move at the time, the torreando guard pass, or "bullfighter." This technique involves pinning the opponent's knees to the mat and gaining bodily control.

Since then, Galvão has mastered a veritable encyclopedia of grappling moves. Rolls, sprawls, grips, throws, arm bars, spins . . . many variations of those and other techniques are second nature to him.

Fighting in the welterweight and middleweight classes, Galvão has won numerous Pan American and world jiu-jitsu championships since 2002. He became a professional MMA fighter in 2008. At the 2011 ADCC Submission Wrestling World Championship, Galvão won gold in both the absolute and 194 pound (88 kilogram) weight classes.

The key elements of Brazilian jiu-jitsu, Galvão believes, are "body movements. In my experience, there is only one way to program these neuromuscular transmissions, and that is through carefully designed drilling and sparring training."

The 5-foot-7-inch (170 centimeters) BJJ black belt teaches Brazilian jiu-jitsu at a San Diego, California, academy and leads the U.S. Atos Jiu-Jitsu team. The 2010 book Galvão coauthored, *Drill to Win: One Year to Better Brazilian Jiu-Jitsu*, encompasses submission wrestling among other skills. It emphasizes the constant need for disciplined physical drills and a healthy diet.

The young fighter believes his spiritual faith is at the root of his success. In his book, he says God "pointed me in the right direction to achieve all my goals. He showed me that hard work will pay off and I just have to focus on what is important in my life." Galvão says this has been true even in his losses and hardships.

FEDOR EMELIANENKO

Emelianenko was born in Rubizhne, Ukraine, in 1976. After graduating from trade school and serving as a firefighter in the army, he began training and competing as a mixed martial artist while in his early twenties.

Emelianenko has won many world and national heavyweight titles in judo, sambo, and mixed martial arts. His crowning triumph was in the 2004 Pride Heavyweight Grand Prix. He also is a four-time world combat sambo champion.

Emelianenko is noted for his versatility as well as his tremendous power. He is feared for his "top game," particularly his ground and

In the opinion of some analysts, Fedor Emelianenko *(top)* is the best mixed martial artist ever to compete. Because of his great strength, he is a submission threat even from positions of disadvantage. In this 2008 match, he is fighting Tim Sylvia.

championship in 2003, while Emelianenko, injured, was absent from fighting. When the two met for a world title fight the following year, Emelianenko was seriously hurt by an unintentional head butt. The bout was stopped with no winner. In December 2004, they fought again, with Emelianenko again winning by decision.

A memorable quick victory was his defeat of highly ranked Tim Sylvia in 2008. Emelianenko immediately floored Sylvia with punches, then submitted him with a rear naked choke. The fight lasted 36 seconds. Sylvia paid his conqueror an interesting tribute: "I don't even think he's human."

A much longer, physically taxing triumph was his Pride championship defense against Mirko "Cro Cop" Filipović in 2005. Filipović broke Emelianenko's nose with a first-round punch and kicked the champîon so savagely that Emelianenko's abdomen was visibly bruised. Superior stamina eventually gave the defender a victory by judges' decision.

pound attacks. But he is also respected for his use of guard techniques and his ability to obtain submission holds while on his back.

Emelianenko has fought several bouts against Antônio Rodrigo Nogueira, another leading MMA contender. At Pride 25, Emelianenko pounded his way to earn a judges' decision. Nogueira won the interim heavyweight

As with many other competitors, injuries have interrupted his career. Emelianenko has been troubled by recurring hand injuries since 2003.

Some MMA observers believe Emelianenko is one of the best—if not the best—mixed-form fighters ever to compete. Emelianenko is also a man of many other interests. He especially enjoys music, literature, and art.

KENNY FLORIAN

Kenny Florian has been a force to compete with as an Ultimate Fighting Championship middleweight, welterweight, lightweight, and featherweight contender. Among other credits, he is the only UFC contender who has competed in four weight divisions.

A master of the Brazilian jiu-jitsu and muay Thai forms, Florian carefully plans his fight strategies. He is feared especially for his submission victories using the rear

Kenny Florian *(left)*, who has won bouts in four of the lighter-weight classes, is known to many MMA television viewers as an expert commentator. He also produces training videos. In this featherweight bout, he is fighting Brazilian Diego Nunes.

naked choke. Florian is also a powerful striker, famous for his sharp, precise elbow blows.

Florian was born to Peruvian parents in 1976 in Westwood, Massachusetts. At a young age, he became proficient at tennis and martial arts. Soccer, however, was his main passion in high school and at

FIGHTING FAMILIES

Many of the world's finest grapplers are from fighting families. André Galvão's brothers Carlos and Gustavo both trained in judo and jiu-jitsu. Kenny Florian runs a martial arts center with his brother Keith, a black belt fighter. Antônio Rodrigo Nogueira's twin brother, Antônio Rogério, is an accomplished mixed martial artist, as are Fedor Emelianenko's brothers Alexander and Ivan.

In 2008, Olympic enthusiasts marveled at the performance of the Lopez family in tae kwon do, a kick-fighting sport. Three Lopez siblings—Mark, Steven, and Diana—won medals for the United States. They were coached by their older brother Jean.

The most prominent MMA lineage is the Gracie family of Brazil—the founding family of Brazilian jiu-jitsu. Over four generations, some three dozen Gracie men and women have earned respect for their BJJ achievements. Probably the family's most accomplished grappler is Royce Gracie.

Boston College, where he played on the varsity team. Florian was an excellent student, making the Boston College dean's list.

He then turned his full attention to mixed martial arts and earned a black belt in Brazilian jiu-jitsu. He understood that in order to succeed in MMA, he would need to master other techniques. As part of his training, he worked with Darryl Gholar, an Olympic coach in Greco-Roman wrestling and an international competitor. Alejo Morales, a one-time coach of the Cuban national wrestling team, was another of his trainers. His improved wrestling skills soon began to pay off.

Florian made a name for himself in 2003 and 2004 at the Mass Destruction 10 and MD 15 events. Over the next several years, he successfully competed in UFC Fight Nights. Many of his victories came by rear naked chokes. But he has also been a victim of the technique, as in his loss to B. J. Penn in a 2009 UFC lightweight title fight.

In February 2011, Florian moved down to the UFC featherweight division. Later that year, he lost a title bid against defending featherweight champion José Aldo. Florian decided to undergo a six-month restrengthening program and return to lightweight competition. By that point, Florian had won fifteen of twenty-one MMA fights; ten of his victories were by submission.

Fighting is only part of Florian's MMA career. He has conducted MMA seminars and produced training DVDs. He has appeared on *The Ultimate Fighter* reality series and as cohost of the weekly *MMA Live* for ESPN.com. He is a frequent television commentator at mixed martial arts events. Florian has appeared on the popular *Dr. Phil* show with other MMA celebrities, warning teenagers against unsupervised MMA fighting.

ANTÔNIO RODRIGO NOGUEIRA

Nogueira, a leading heavyweight Ultimate Fighting Championship contender, is a technical master of MMA. Because of his exceptional physical build, he has been called "the Bull."

During the late 1990s, he won national and Pan American championships in Brazilian jiu-jitsu. He made the quarter-final round of the ADCC World Submission Wrestling Championships. Nogueira then entered the MMA arena. He launched his reputation by winning the heavyweight division of the Japanese Pride Fighting Championships in 2001–2002.

Born in Vitoria da Conquista, Brazil, in 1974, Nogueira was only four when he began learning judo. When he was ten, he almost died after being hit by a truck. Nogueira was hospitalized for almost a year and suffered permanent internal injuries.

The injuries did not stifle his desire to excel as a disciplined fighter. As a teenager, he first took up boxing, then Brazilian jiu-jitsu. He earned his BJJ black belt in 1999.

Nogueira was awarded "Fighter of the Year" honors in 2002 by *Wrestling Observer Newsletter*

Antônio Rodrigo Nogueira became a world-class MMA contender despite a childhood injury that resulted in long-term hospitalization and permanent physical challenges. Inside the cage, he is dubbed "the Bull."

has won the UFC "Knockout of the Night" once and "Fight of the Night" contests twice. He defeated Randy Couture, a long-time MMA superstar, in a 2009 UFC fight that observers rate as one of the epic struggles of all time.

Nogueira won Pride 15 by using a triangle choke to submit his opponent. At Pride 16, he won with an arm bar. Since then, he has used chokes and arm bars repeatedly in his victories. He won two important matches in 2004 with an original move he developed, the anaconda choke.

His most famous fight was against Bob Sapp in 2002. Sapp, a 6-foot-5-inch (196–cm), 350-pound (159-kg) former professional football player and wrestler, is called "the Beast." His pounding style is especially punishing even by MMA standards. Because of their size difference (Nogueira stood 2 inches (5 cm) shorter and was more than a hundred pounds lighter), the event was dubbed a modern "David and Goliath" battle. Nogueira was struck mercilessly. However, he managed to withstand the storm of blows until

and *Black Belt Magazine*. He joined the UFC in 2007. Besides his Pride titles, Nogueira has been interim UFC heavyweight champion. He

Sapp began to tire. Then he secured a classic arm bar to win the match.

Among Nogueira's interesting achievements outside the cage is acting. He was cast as a soldier in the 2010 film *The Expendables*.

RANDY COUTURE

A retired former heavyweight and light-heavyweight MMA champion, Randy Couture is legendary. During his years of competition, he was noted for his chokeholds and clinches. He was also famous for using short punches in combination with his wrestling prowess to perfect a style referred to as "dirty boxing."

A native of Everett, Washington, Couture was born in 1963. He describes himself as a "fearless" and "curious" child. When he was four, excited by a cowboy-and-Indian fight scene on TV, he stabbed himself with a paring knife to find out what it felt like.

Not surprisingly, Couture took an early interest in combat sports, becoming a

Multiple champion Randy Couture earned the respect of everyone in MMA for his determination as well as his skill. Most of his fights were against larger opponents. Couture officially retired from MMA fighting in 2011.

scholastic wrestler. He was a member of his middle school wrestling team and in high school won a Washington State wrestling championship.

After serving in the army, Couture became a wrestling coach. He was also an NCAA all-American wrestler. Between 1988 and 2000, he came just short of making Olympic wrestling teams four times. But in the early 1990s, his interest turned to mixed martial arts.

Couture is small for a heavyweight—6 feet 1 inch (185 cm) tall, just over 200 pounds (91 kg). He frequently was the underdog, but he usually found ways to win. In his first MMA tournament in 1997, both of his opponents outweighed him by almost 100 pounds (45.4 kg). He defeated one with a rear naked choke, the other by technical knockout.

His personal style, cleverly blending jabs with grappling, was unique. Couture was a leading ground and pound fighter—boxing, kneeing, and elbowing the opponent while in a full mount. He was one of the most effective clinchers in MMA. His jabbing while in clinches helped him confuse opponents and set up leg trips and other takedowns. He usually ended up in the full mount position, his opponent in deep trouble.

Couture won the UFC heavyweight championship three times and the light-heavyweight championship twice. He contended in fifteen UFC championship fights—the most of any UFC competitor. At forty-three, he became the oldest UFC fighter to win a title. He was an obvious selection for membership in the UFC Hall of Fame.

Wrestling Observer Newsletter named Couture the "MMA Most Valuable Fighter" in 2007. The publication later pronounced him the "MMA Most Valuable Fighter of the Decade."

Couture retired in 2011. Observers consider him among the handful of leading fighters who have lifted mixed martial arts to mainstream sport status. Couture is also an author and actor.

CHAPTER 3

GRAPPLING TECHNIQUES STEP-BY-STEP

"To win one-hundred victories in one hundred battles is not the highest skill. To defeat the enemy without fighting is the highest skill."— Sun-tzu

The techniques illustrated here are important for grapplers to master. They are seen not only at grappling competitions but at most MMA events. Essential to grappling are clinches, takedowns, submission techniques, and defenses against every attack.

To a reader who never has tried them, some grappling moves may appear easy to execute. It takes much training to perform them successfully in combat, though. It requires years of training and experience to incorporate them effortlessly into a fighter's repertoire and learn to use them in combination with other moves.

Training academies and gyms in cities and towns across the country teach grappling techniques. Instruction is available for adults and children. Most facilities offer demonstrations and trial lessons. Some schools specialize in one form of martial arts, such as jiu-jitsu or grappling. Others offer courses in multiple forms.

Keep in mind that the methods and moves provided here are intended for self-defense and fitness. Young people who want to learn more about what is involved in grappling and submission grappling should look to local training centers or qualified private instructors. Videos and instruction books are useful study tools for mastering MMA, but techniques cannot be learned properly without hands-on guidance. A beginner should find an instructor who teaches all aspects of the sport: discipline, physical fitness, diet, a respectful attitude, and—especially—safety.

CLINCH

Start in a fighting stance parallel to your opponent. Bend both knees.

Start to develop momentum. Shoot for opponent's chest area.

Wrap arms around opponent's chest area, as if you were giving him a hug, and grab your left wrist with your right hand. Collapse your torso. Make sure your head is buried slightly inside your right arm/shoulder.

SINGLE-LEG TAKEDOWN

Starting in a fighting stance parallel to your opponent, shoot for opponent's front leg. Do this motion by bending both knees.

Develop momentum by getting low to the ground, and protect your face by staying in your fighting stance. Have your shoulders parallel with opponent's shins.

DOUBLE-LEG TAKEDOWN

28

Beginning in a fighting stance parallel to your opponent, shoot for both of your opponent's legs. Do this motion by bending both knees.

Develop momentum by getting low to the ground, and protect your face by staying in your fighting stance.

Put your front knee in somewhat of a 90-degree angle with your foot on the ground. Simultaneously, shift hips forward as your rear knee touches ground. This is called a "duck walk."

Instantaneously, align your left shoulder parallel with opponent's front ankle. Clasp hands over one another (all ten fingers) behind opponent's ankle/Achilles tendon. Shift your body weight to your shoulder and drive forward.

Clinch back of both of opponent's knees. Make sure to clinch by clasping all ten of your fingers together behind opponent's knees.

Collapse both of opponent's knees. Your head is positioned tightly to opponent's body. Drive forward with front shoulder.

As you see your opponent coming fast and closely for a takedown, scoot your rear leg backward. Straighten leg as much as you can.

Angle your hips and rear backward and up. If opponent tries to grab your front leg, straighten front leg out. In this position, both legs are sprawled, hips elevated to ceiling. Clinch opponent's torso.

FIREMAN'S CARRY

While in a fighting stance, bend both knees and become parallel with opponent's hips. Close space between you and your opponent.

Position right arm underneath and between opponent's legs. Make sure right arm wraps all the way up opponent's lower back.

HIP THROW

While in a fighting stance, bend both knees and become parallel with opponent's hips. Close space between you and your opponent.

Position right arm underneath opponent's left shoulder and keep snug.

Grab opponent's right wrist with your left hand. Use your right shoulder and swing hips so right hip moves forward and left hip moves back.

Grab opponent's right wrist with your left hand. Shift your rear to the right and position it to opponent's hip. Make sure your feet are positioned inside opponent's feet.

Swing hips so right hip moves forward and left hip moves back. Throw opponent as if you were chopping wood.

HIP THROW INTO ARM BAR

In a fighting stance, bend both knees and become parallel with opponent's hips. Close space between you and your opponent.

Position right arm underneath opponent's left shoulder and keep snug. Grab opponent's right wrist with your left hand. Shift your rear to the right and position it to opponent's hip. Make sure your feet are positioned inside opponent's feet.

Swing hips so right hip moves forward and left hip moves back. Throw opponent as if you were chopping wood.

As you are throwing opponent, hold onto his left hand as his back hits the floor. Position right knee toward ceiling and inside opponent's armpit. Position your left knee across opponent's chest.

Squeeze your knees together. Raise pelvis to the ceiling. Have opponent's thumb facing ceiling. You're now submitting the opponent in the arm bar.

BROOM SWEEP FROM CLINCH INTO MOUNT

Bend both knees. Start to develop momentum. Shoot for opponent's chest area. Wrap arms around opponent's chest area, as if you are giving him a hug, and grab your left wrist with your right hand.

Collapse torso. Make sure your head is buried slightly inside your right arm/shoulder. Now you have the opponent in your clinch.

AMERICANA FROM MOUNT

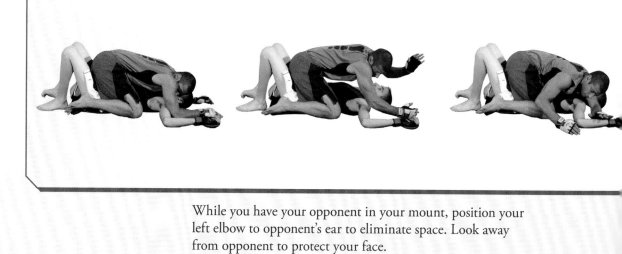

While you have your opponent in your mount, position your left elbow to opponent's ear to eliminate space. Look away from opponent to protect your face.

Position your left foot behind opponent's right heel. Sweep right foot like a broom as head pushes in at the same time. This creates more momentum. Drive opponent to floor.

As opponent falls to floor, follow his momentum. Swing knee across belly and pin to opponent's left hip. You now have the opponent in your mount.

Your left hand goes underneath opponent's arm and grabs your own wrist. Opponent's arm never comes off the ground.

Sweep opponent's arm like a "broom" while opponent's elbow is being slightly maneuvered toward ceiling. You're now submitting the opponent in the Americana.

ARM DRAG INTO SLEEPER HOLD

Protect your face from opponent. Pick a side and commit to it. If picking opponent's left side, quickly grab opponent's right wrist with your left hand. Position your right hand underneath opponent's right triceps. Pull opponent toward you. (Think of it as pulling a rope toward you, as in a tug-of-war.)

As opponent swings toward you, position your left hand around opponent's left hip. Swing your right leg around opponent's hip and wrap your right foot underneath opponent's right calf. This motion is a hook.

Once you hook the opponent's right leg, you will now put your hook in with your left leg. Make sure there's no space between your hips and opponent's back.

Bring right arm underneath opponent's chin all the way to the point of where your elbow is aligned and parallel with opponent's chin.

Have your right hand come all the way up to your left shoulder, as this creates more pressure. Your left hand is positioned behind opponent's head for defense against head butts.

Squeeze both elbows in toward one another. You're now submitting the opponent in the sleeper hold. Apply more pressure by putting your head against opponent's head.

GLOSSARY

aikido An ancient martial art that blends grappling with striking techniques.

arm bar A type of submission technique in which the elbow is hyperextended (forced against its natural bending motion).

Brazilian jiu-jitsu The ancient art of jiu-jitsu as perfected by the Gracie family in Brazil.

clinch To struggle for advantage at close quarters, usually in a standing position at the beginning of a fight.

Greco-Roman wrestling A form of wrestling believed to be based on the grappling styles of classical Greece and Rome.

jiu-jitsu A fighting system of throws, holds, and blows renowned for redirecting an opponent's strengths. (Also spelled jujitsu.)

judo Derived from jiu-jitsu, judo ("gentle way") emphasizes personal growth in training.

kung fu Any of various ancient Chinese fighting systems that emphasize personal skill levels.

mount A controlling position in which a fighter straddles the opponent's midsection.

Pride A Japanese-based organization that sponsored MMA world championships and other major events from 1997 to 2007.

sambo A form of grappling perfected in Russia.

sparring A part of training in which a fighter competes and practices techniques with a skilled opponent.

sprawl A defense effected by firmly spreading the legs.

submission Applying a grappling technique that forces an opponent to give up (submit).

sumo A Japanese wrestling form in which no part of the body except the feet may touch the ground.

sweeps Techniques used to unbalance an opponent or to reverse an inferior position.

tae kwon do A Korean system of martial arts based on kicking.

t'ai chi An ancient Chinese system of meditative movements.

takedown The act of taking an opponent to the ground.

throw Any of a number of moves using arms, legs, or hips to throw an opponent to the ground.

wrestling Generally, fighting by grappling; modern professional wrestling is a form of entertainment.

FOR MORE INFORMATION

Canadian Grappling & Striking Sports Council
18 Acton Court
London, ON N6E W5
Canada
(647) 668-8472
Web site: http://http://www.cgssc.com
Coordinates and promotes events and fosters sportsmanship.

Canadian National Martial Arts Association
1-3946 Quadra Street
Victoria, BC V8X 16J
Canada
Web site: http://cnmaa.com
Promotes martial arts nationwide through competition,
   physical activities, and community

Gracie Barra
14988 Sand Canyon Avenue, Studio 1
Irvine, CA 92618
(949) 795-5257
Web Site: http://www.graciebarraamerica.com
Gracie Barra is the U.S. headquarters of one of the larg-
   est and most traditional Brazilian jiu-jitsu schools in
   the world. Carlos Gracie Jr. is the founder and head
   instructor.

Gracie Jiu-Jitsu Academy
3515 Artesia Boulevard
Torrance, CA 90504
(877) 472-2430
Web Site: http://www.gracieacademy.com
This is the U.S. headquarters for the famous Gracie Academy.

International Brazilian Jiu-Jitsu Federation
Av Comandante Júlio de Moura 276
Barra da Tijuca
Rio de Janeiro, RJ 22620-012
Brazil
Web Site: http://www.ibjjf.org
This federation was created by Carlos Gracie Jr. to
   represent the sport of Brazilian jiu-jitsu around
   the world.

International Federation of Associated Wrestling (FILA)
Rue du Château, 6-1804 Corsier-sur-Vevey
Switzerland
Web site: http://www.fila-wrestling.com
The organization establishes rules and organizes events in
   different styles of wrestling around the world.

Judo Canada

212 - 1725 St. Laurent
Ottawa, ON K1G 3V4
Canada
(613)-738-1200
Web Site: http://www.judocanada.org
Judo Canada is the national governing body for the sport of
judo in Canada.

Krav Maga Worldwide

11400 Olympic Boulevard, Suite 100
Los Angeles, CA 90064
(310) 966-1300
Web site: http://www.kravmaga.com
An organization created in 1999 by Darren Levine,
6th-degree black belt and recipient of a Founder's
Diploma from Krav Maga creator Imi Lichtenfeld,
to help spread Krav Maga training across the United
States and around the globe.

Muay Thai Association of America (MTAA)

11116 Weddington Street
North Hollywood, CA 91601
(818) 980-6688
Web Site: http://www.muaythaiassociation
ofamerica.com
The MTAA promotes the art of muay Thai in the
United States.

North American Grappling Association

36 Saner Road
Marlborough, CT 06447
(860) 295-0403
Web site: http://www.nagafighter.com
An organizer of grappling tournaments in North America.

United States Martial Arts Association

8011 Mariposa Avenue
Citrus Heights, CA 95610-1514
(916) 727-1486
Web site: http://www.marrts.org
Nonprofit organization dedicated to unifying MMA in the
United States. It provides seminars, training camps, and
other resources.

WEB SITES

Due to the changing nature of Internet links, Rosen
Publishing has developed an online list of Web sites
related to the subject of this book. This site is up-
dated regularly. Please use this link to access the list:

http://www.rosenlinks.com/mma/sub

FOR FURTHER READING

Ellis, Carol. *Judo and Jujitsu* (Martial Arts in Action). New York, NY: Benchmark Books, 2011.

Freeman, Gary. *Self-Defense* (Instant Expert). North Mankato, MN: Capstone Press, 2011.

Haines, Lise. *Girl in the Arena*. New York, NY: Bloomsbury USA, 2010.

Haney, Johannah. *Capoeira* (Martial Arts in Action). New York, NY: Benchmark Books, 2011.

Jones, Brian. *Grappling Basics: A New Twist on Conditioning*. Nevada City, CA: IronMind Enterprises, 2008.

Kimpel, Steve. *Wrestle and Win: The Wrestler's Guide to Strength, Conditioning, Nutrition and College Preparation*. Santa Fe, NM: Turtle Press, 2010.

Kreidler, Mark. *Four Days to Glory: Wrestling with the Soul of the American Heartland*. New York, NY: Harper Paperbacks, 2007.

Ollhoff, Jim. *Grappling* (The World of Martial Arts). Edina, MN: ABDO Publishing, 2008.

Ollhoff, Jim. *Martial Arts Around the Globe* (The World of Martial Arts). Edina, MN: ABDO Publishing, 2008.

Scandiffio, Laura. *The Martial Arts Book*. Toronto, ON, Canada: Annick Press, 2010.

Wells, Garrison. *Amateur Wrestling: Combat on the Mat* (Martial Arts Sports Zone). Minneapolis, MN: Lerner Publishing Group, 2012.

Wells, Garrison. *Mixed Martial Arts: Ultimate Fighting Combinations* (Martial Arts Sports Zone). Minneapolis, MN: Lerner Publishing Group, 2012.

Wiseman, Blaine. *Martial Arts* (In the Zone). New York, NY: Weigl Publishers, 2010.

Wiseman, Blaine. *Ultimate Fighting* (Sporting Championships). New York, NY: Weigl Publishers, 2010.

BIBLIOGRAPHY

Adams, Mike. "Why Mixed Martial Arts Is Good for Children (Opinion)." NaturalNews.com. Retrieved November 17, 2011 (http://www.naturalnews.com/023000_Chi_child_children.html).

Bearak, Barry. "Ultimate Fighting Dips a Toe Into the Mainstream." *New York Times*, November 12, 2011. Retrieved November 12, 2011 (http://www.nytimes.com/2011/11/12/sports/ultimate-fighting-championship-comes-of-age-financially.html?_r=1@ref=todayspaper).

BJJ Heroes. "Andre Galvao (Atos)." February 7, 2010. Retrieved November 9, 2011 (http://www.bjjheroes.com/bjj-fightersandre-galvao-bjj-and-mma-fighter-wiki).

Corcoran, John. "Martial Arts." Microsoft Student 2008 (DVD). Redmond, WA: Microsoft Corporation, 2007.

Couture, Randy, with Loretta Hunt. *Becoming the Natural: My Life In and Out of the Cage*. New York, NY: Simon Spotlight Entertainment (a division of Simon & Schuster, Inc.), 2008.

Dimic, Mickey. *Mixed Martial Arts Unleashed: Mastering the Most Effective Moves for Victory*. New York, NY: McGraw-Hill, 2009.

Galvão, André, with Kevin Howell. *Drill to Win: 12 Months to Better Brazilian Jiu-Jitsu*. Las Vegas, NV: Victory Belt Publishing, 2010.

Goldman, John. *Guide to Martial Arts*. New York, NY: Todtri Productions Limited, 1997.

Krauss, Erich. *The Ultimate Mixed Martial Artist: The Fighter's Manual to Striking Combinations, Takedowns, the Clinch, and Cage Tactics*. Las Vegas, NV: Victory Belt Publishing, 2009.

Krueger, Ray. "Times Topics: Mixed Martial Arts." *New York Times*. Retrieved November 21, 2011 (http://topics.nytimes.com/top/reference/

timestopics/subjects/m/mixed_martial_arts/
index.html?inline=nyt-classifier).

Lopez, Mark, et al. *Family Power: The True Story
of How "The First Family of Taekwondo" Made
Olympic History*. New York, NY: Celebra (New
American Library), 2009.

Pearlman, Steven J. *The Book of Martial Power:
The Universal Guide to the Combative Arts*.
Woodstock, NY: The Overlook Press, 2006.

Sandomir, Richard. "U.F.C. Sues State Over
Ban on Mixed Martial Arts Bouts." *New
York Times*, November 15, 2011. Retrieved
November 15, 2011 (http://www.nytimes.
com/2011/11/16/sports/ufc-sues-to-lift-new-
york-ban-on-mixed-martial-arts-fighting.
html?_r=1&ref=todayspaper).

Sidney, James, ed. *The Warrior's Path: Wisdom from
Contemporary Martial Arts Masters*. Boston,
MA: Shambala Publications, Inc., 2003.

Snowden, Jonathan, and Kendall Shields. *The MMA
Encyclopedia*. Toronto, ON: ECW Press, 2010.

Wertheim, L. Jon. *Blood in the Cage: Mixed
Martial Arts, Pat Miletich, and the Furious Rise
of the UFC*. Boston, MA: Houghton Mifflin
Harcourt, 2009.

INDEX

A
Abu Dhabi Combat Club, 12
agility, 13
Americana, 13, 36–37
arm bar, 13, 16, 22, 23, 34–35
arm drag, 12, 38–39
arm lock, 13

B
broom sweep, 36–37

C
chokes, 5, 13, 18, 19, 20, 22, 23, 24
clinches, 8, 10, 23, 25, 26–27, 29,
    30–31, 36
Couture, Randy, 22, 23–24

D
diet, 13–14, 17, 26
double-leg throw, 11, 12, 28–29

E
Emelianenko, Fedor, 17–19, 20

F
falls, 12

fireman's carry, 11, 32–33
Florian, Kenny, 19–21

G
Galvão, André, 13–14, 15, 16–17, 20
Gracie family, 20
guard techniques, 12

H
hip throw, 11, 32–33, 34–35

I
International Federation of Associated
    Wrestling Styles (FILA), 7, 12

L
leg sweep, 11
limb locks, 13
Lopez family, 20

M
mounts, 11–12, 13, 24, 36–37

N
Nogueira, Antônio Rodrigo, 18, 20, 21–23

R
rear naked choke, 13, 18, 19, 20, 24
rolls, 12, 13, 16

S
side mount, 11, 13
single-leg throw, 11, 28–29
sleeper hold, 38–39
sprawls, 12, 16, 30–31
strangles, 13
strength training, 13
Submission Wrestling World
    Championship, 12, 17

T
takedowns, 10–12, 15, 24, 25,
    28–29, 30, 32–33
throws, 5, 11, 12, 28–29, 32–33
training, 13–14, 20, 25

ABOUT THE AUTHOR

Daniel E. Harmon has written more than seventy books, including numerous works on health and fitness topics. He is a veteran magazine and newspaper editor and writer whose articles have appeared in many national and regional periodicals.

ABOUT BEN DANIEL

Ben Daniel was born in Israel and raised in Margate, New Jersey. He has a bachelor of science degree in biology from Richard Stockton College of New Jersey. He has been training under Master Mal Perkins in American tae kwon do since age six and has also practiced Brazilian jiu-jitsu and hapkido each for nine years. Since receiving his first-degree black belt at the age of sixteen, he has been teaching martial arts to students of all ages. He is now a third-degree black belt and is in training for his fourth-degree master's belt. He resides in New York, where he works as a professional personal trainer.

PHOTO CREDITS

Cover (left), p. 1 (left) Jon Kopaloff/FilmMagic/Getty Images; p. 4 Jon P. Kopaloff/Getty Images; p. 6 Cris Bouroncle/AFP/Getty Images; pp. 9, 10, 16, 19, 23 © AP Images; p. 14 Joel Saget/AFP/Getty Images; p. 18 Francis Specker/Landov; p. 22 SMI/Newscom; cover and interior background graphics and textures © iStockphoto,com/ranplett (canvas), Ana de Sousa/Shutterstock.com (wall), © iStockphoto.com/Arena Creative (fence); cover (right), pp. 1 (right), 8, 15, 25, and all photos on pages 26–39 by Cindy Reiman, assisted by Karen Huang.

Designer: Brian Garvey; Editor: Kathy Kuhtz Campbell; Photo Researcher: Karen Huang